BE A MORTGAGE SALES HERO

Up Your Game, Close More Loans, and Be a Borrower's Hero in the Mortgage Call Center Industry

MORGAN SOKOL

ISBN-13: 978-1720735069
ISBN-10: 1720735069

Publishing Consulting – Tracy Paye
Book Layout/Production – Tracy Paye
Cover Design – Belladia Marketing and Design
Contact: info@beamortgagesaleshero.com

Table of Contents

TESTIMONIALS

"Morgan had a strong reputation for building successful mortgage teams that preceded our first conversation. We brought him on board as one of the leads in the creation of an ambitious call center. His sales acumen, dedication, and solid work ethic showed us his ability to turn our call center into a successful endeavor."
– Adam Wagner, Senior Vice President

"I just wanted to let you know that when we thought all hope was lost when trying to get our refinance completed, Morgan stepped in and saved the day. He is an asset to your organization, and my wife and I are very grateful."
– Borrower

"In the direct-to-consumer mortgage industry, Morgan has achieved excellence as both an originator and a sales manager. He knows what it takes to be a top-producing loan officer. As a sales

manager, he exemplifies the skill set necessary to get the best from his people. Listen to Sokol, and you will make money!"
– Tom Redmond, Mortgage Professional since 1987

"Within a few months of being personally trained by Morgan, I was top 10 in the company and number-three in our branch, constantly closing every month and ending my year and each year after with record-breaking income. If you're willing to be open-minded and apply his wealth of call center knowledge, your odds of success will multiply."
– Daniel Curtis, Team Lead

"Under Morgan Sokol, I had my best year ever in my 15 years in the mortgage industry. He is very detailed in his daily work tasks. He was a big reason why I was able to make the Chairman's Club for the first time in my career. Morgan was very good about keeping me motivated to do better. If you are able to take anything away from this material, you will be a better person and professional for it."

– Michael Domico, Loan Officer since 2000

ACKNOWLEDGMENTS

Life, for beating me down at times but allowing me to get back up, which is not always easy but necessary.

Don Ruff, who saw something in me that others may not have and allowed me to move up to my first management position in the mortgage industry. Hang in there, buddy. We are rootin' for you to get better.

My Old Man, who, despite being a pain in my side sometimes, has through the years always given me sage advice that has helped in many different areas. Many a night was spent sleeping in his office, which taught me about work ethic.

Most of all, **Tracy Paye**, who motivated and assisted me in putting all my thoughts and training over the years into writing. Without her support, this book would never have been.

PREFACE

If you have ever met a successful loan officer who told you their job is always easy, congratulations! You have just located a golden unicorn leaping into a pile of cash and well-aged whisky.

I've worked wretched sales jobs in other industries that made me want to cry big sloppy tears and hit sweet little babies. Thankfully, I'm not into either.

Mortgage sales can be a rough gig. I mean, it can be soul-crushing. You are right at the finish line and ready to fund that loan that has been in processing for four months with the borrower who is in bad financial shape but who you are the biggest cheerleader for. They lost their job a few years ago and spent the rest of their savings taking care of their kid who has cancer. Then the hammer drops, and underwriting finds a mystery lien on the property, that second on the county-funded solar energy system they added and forgot about that the county won't subordinate. After all that work on both ends, the refinance just got buried six feet under. It's a feeling only a loan officer can understand.

If you've been in the mortgage profession for more than a week, you've said to yourself, likely more than once, *"I don't know if I can do this anymore."* Still, you push on for a variety of reasons, most of which are based on financial gain. However, financial gain shouldn't be your only reason, because if it is and you know what you're offering is detrimental to the client, then you will both lose in the end. It's just not good for the soul.

We are in a great industry, sometimes a life-changing industry, for both the loan officer and the client. You should respect and appreciate that. However, there is no silver bullet in our industry. Your sales success must be earned.

The mortgage industry can have more moving parts than the Terminator (T3 version), and the Council for Fair Business Practices (CFPB) seems to think you've already done something wrong before you've written your first 1003.

Typically, people are not fans of rules, but they are necessary. In this book, I'm going to attempt to provide a few to follow in one area that continues to grow and be profitable: call center mortgage sales. I will primarily deal with refinancing, but the tools presented are also applicable to purchase loans.

Fact: **Every person in every profession is selling something.** If you're in information technology (IT), you're selling your tech skills. If you're a barber, you're selling your cuttin' hair skills.

For some people, earning money through hard work is out of the question. I hate to be the old man yelling, *"Get off my lawn!"* but I see this attitude more frequently in the 20- to early 30-somethings. These attitudes can be really irritating, especially when they're making $100k+ and telling me that the 40-hour-a-week job is affecting their social lives. Seriously, it is mind-numbing. A big fall is what it's going to take for them to realize that they had it pretty good, a fall that I took myself.

When I was around 30, I was feeling somewhat cocky. I had months when I was making over $30k; I owned a condo by the beach, drove a convertible Porsche, and had just bought a giant investment property in Las Vegas.

I naïvely assumed I'd buy a house every year and have liquid millions in the bank within 10 years. It felt like I was hitting 21 at the tables non-stop! That's called being arrogant and short-sighted, folks.

Then it happened—that mighty '08 financial storm from hell. Within six months, I went from livin' the dream to working for a hideous loan-mod company. Oh, how the mighty (my own ego, that is) had fallen.

I once worked 33 days straight, including Sundays, in 2011 and made a whopping $2k. The job was terrible, and I was miserable. I lost everything in the blink of an eye: my houses, my car, my money, and my self-respect.

With everything wrapped up, I declared bankruptcy for over a million dollars. Let's just say Wells Fargo wasn't my biggest fan. More importantly, I lost my self-esteem and confidence. Every crappy debt settlement or loan modification company I worked for seemed to go insolvent and stiff me. Some of the owners appeared to be, and in some cases were, crooks.

I once worked for a loan-mod company where the owner, who was a steroid-takin', Bentley-drivin' piece of work, bragged about knocking out an employee for stealing leads and threatened us if we did the same. No, this wasn't 1911; it was 2011. I was scrambling to survive, and I didn't want to believe that what I was selling borrowers was garbage, yet subconsciously, I knew it was.

I felt mediocre, and that added to my depression. I couldn't see any way out of the mess, and I wasn't alone. Most of my fellow loan officers went from Dom Perignon bottle service to 40oz. bottles of Olde English.

Nevertheless, through a ton of hard work, I made it through and became better in sales and overall a better human being because of the experience. My intention for this book is to share my experience, knowledge, and insight so you too can have a successful career in mortgages and specifically the mortgage call center industry. Each of these concepts I review could almost be a separate book in itself; however, I did not want to rewrite *Atlas*

Shrugged, so I tried to keep them succinct and to the point.

QUOTES

"We cannot change the cards we are dealt, just how we play the hand." – Randy Pausch

"For every sale you miss because you're too enthusiastic, you will miss a hundred because you're not enthusiastic enough." – Zig Ziglar

"Don't watch the clock; do what it does. Keep going." – Sam Levenson

Chapter 1

THE SKINNY

Why are you sitting in a cubicle for hours on end, staring at a computer and sometimes having to deal with borrowers who treat you as if you stole their tasty turkey sammy with avocado out of the work fridge? Money. That's why.

Let's face it: Most of us don't have some philanthropic reason to get into the mortgage biz.

Either we want that new car, a new house, or to provide for our families, or more importantly, we can't wait to jump in the freaky crazy-dome at the next Burning Man.

Regardless of your reasons, a few basics are absolute necessities. You need to understand that in selling a mortgage, you are improving the borrower's life. It's not sleazy as sometimes perceived—it's awesome. Good loan officers understand this. Bad or mediocre ones do not, and they suffer because of it. The bottom line is that selling a mortgage is a win-win: You and the borrower both gain financially in some aspect. Whether it be a refinance or a purchase, either can be life-changing or life-saving. Both parties should be happy once the transaction is completed. If you are padding your bank account, you have nothing to feel guilty about if you did your job properly and within compliance—both parties benefited from the transaction.

Unfortunately, some borrowers still have the stink of pre-2008 on them, and loan officers are sometimes seen as necessary villains. In fact, we are in a very regulated (understatement of the year) industry. Our conversations are recorded; everything and anything is in writing. If we continue to slip up, it's only a matter time before Johnny Law—i.e., the CFPB—will end our careers.

I once knew a fellow loan officer who got fired for signing e-documents for a borrower. The borrower couldn't figure out how to sign, so the loan officer asked the borrower if it was okay if he signed for him. The loan officer told the borrower that they were on a recorded line, asked the borrower to verify, and directly after signing, sent him the e-docs. Doesn't matter; can't do it. When the signing was discovered, the loan officer was immediately terminated.

Bottom line: Now isn't 2007. No one is selling loans whose payments are going to change radically in two to three years. Option arms come to mind. The crazy thing is, I sold a ton of option arms (look 'em up, newbies), not knowing of course everything would crash, and afterwards, I felt guilty thinking that they would lead a lot of people into foreclosure.

Here's what happened. The economy was so terrible that the mortgage indexes were mostly held low. Most people had 2% rates for eight years and are still in the 3–4% range. My dad had 1.4%. He thought that I was just writing all subprime loans. The SOB went with someone else because he didn't think I originated them, and the other guy made a $20k commission from it. I wasn't sure how to take that, Pops!

I gave up trying to predict rates. If a borrower asks, I usually say I'm right about 50% of the time, and I think even that's a stretch. With our political and economic climate, things can change on a dime.

TAKEAWAYS

1. Don't lose sight of the fact that what you're doing can change lives for the better.

2. A dirty loan officer would have trouble selling loans in the current environment. A benefit needs to be provided, and the loans must always be compliant.

3. Find out what is best for the borrower. You want to make money on every loan, but do not let profit cloud your judgement.

QUOTES

"Confidence and enthusiasm are the greatest sales producers in any kind of economy." – OB Smith

"If you are not taking care of your customer, your competitor will." – Bob Hooey

Chapter 2

YOUR CONFIDENCE RUNS THE CALL

Whether it's your first time picking up the phone fresh from your National Mortgage Licensing System (NMLS) test or you're a seasoned vet, if you don't have confidence in what you're selling, you're dead in the water before you even open your mouth. So how do you build that confidence?

One essential aspect in mortgage sales is knowing your stuff. Yes, I know there are so many mind-numbing guidelines, you would have to be Rain

Man to remember them all. However, knowing the most common guidelines and products will make even the new blood sound like a pro. In the current climate, we don't have as many funky loans. No 50-year terms with an interest-only option, and yes, that was a loan at one point. Just starting with the basics and continuing to learn makes a huge difference.

When I was a sales manager, it always amazed me as well as tested my patience when a loan officer constantly asked me the same questions. How has this person been selling loans for 30 years without knowing this answer, and how do they continue not to know it? Why are you asking me for the fourth time if a borrower needs to send in his social security card for a Veterans Affairs (VA) loan? The answer is simple: These loan officers are looking five feet in front of them instead of 500. Asking a question is easy; learning the answer to the question takes a bit more effort but will pay dividends. If you have fallen behind, go Rodney

Dangerfield style and get "Back to School!" Hone your art—sales is indeed an art.

I advise my loan officers to look up the answer and then create a separate Excel document or something similar with the answer for reference. Looking a question up and saving the answer tattoos the information on your brain versus asking your neighbor or the boss. There's nothing wrong with asking questions; however, asking the same question over and over and not retaining the knowledge does no one any good. Furthermore, the quick-fix approach makes you appear to be on the job for the short term rather than looking to build a career at your chosen workplace.

ASSUME THE SALE

An important part of closing the loan is to ASSUME the borrower wants to do it. (This may be the only time that assuming something won't make an ass out of—well, you know the saying.)

"Okay, Mr. Borrower, we're saving you $150 a month. This is $9,000 over a period of five years. Your fees for the transaction will be $3,100, and they're wrapped into the loan. What I'm going to do is ask you a few regulatory questions, and after the documents are signed, we should have this wrapped up for you in 30 to 45 days."

Don't say, *"What we can do for you? How does that sound? Does it look good?"* etc. Instead, use assumptive terms like *"What we are going to do,"* *"This is what I need you to do,"* etc. When they hear these assumptive terms, borrowers subconsciously think that this is something that they should be doing. People sometimes need to be led. If you continually pause and ask, *"How does that sound?"* the borrower typically hesitates and decides that this is something that they should take time to consider. Nothing is wrong with taking a client's temperature during the conversation, but if you do it repeatedly, you will start to sound suspect.

What are the six words no loan officer likes to hear? *"Let me think about it."* By not using assumptive terms, you may be leading borrowers to believe that they're supposed to think about the offer. Instead, borrowers should be thinking, *"I'm saving money," "Seems like a pretty easy process,"* and *"This loan officer really seems to be a champ."* (By the way, *"Let me think about it"* is five words; were you paying attention?)

PERSEVERANCE PAYS OFF

The highest-paid loan officer in the office is not always the best salesman. However, successful loan officers take advantage of opportunities. Overtime available? Done. Work on Saturday? I'll be there. I don't think any quality is as essential to success of any kind as the quality of perseverance. Perseverance overcomes almost everything—even nature. There is no shortcut—you must put in the work.

If you work strictly nine-to-five, chances are you're not in the top 10% in your office. Seize every opportunity you can now that overtime is mandated pay for call center jockeys. At a minimum, you'll get paid a few extra bucks.

For a year before the overtime law was in effect, I used to work 10 to 12 hours every day, and I worked at least a few hours every Saturday, with one exception—after a wedding I went to the night before. I think you know what might have happened there. People thought I was insane working so much, but I knew I was never going back to that giant turd sandwich of a situation I faced when the market collapsed.

At one time, I could not speak at all for an entire week. Let's just say I brushed my teeth, and it wasn't toothpaste: My buddy's wife had some Retin-A that looked very similar to a tube of toothpaste, and it basically bleached my vocal cords. I was staying at their house—if anyone was wondering why I was using my buddy's wife's toothpaste, how dare you. Anyways, I missed one day of work, but I showed up the other four mute and managed to be the second-highest producer in the office that week. That was some ninja stuff there.

At the end of the year, I had a lot to show for my perseverance. Out of 140 loan officers on my side of the fence, I was sitting at #1. Those sitting on the couch watching *South Park* reruns were in a different spot. Everyone has personal obligations. However, if your plans are either to lie on the couch or work, **I strongly advise you** to choose work. Get that fire in your belly; you will look back at the end of the year and be thankful that you did. I don't know anyone who has worked their tail off, made more money, and accomplished their goals who has said, *"I wish I had worked less."* This work ethic might cause your significant others to be ticked off, but take 'em to Cabo and jump on a booze cruise with your cash, and all will be forgiven. Embrace the grind, and it, in the end, will embrace you.

CONTROLLING THE CALL

You lead the conversation, not the borrower, period! In this seriously competitive environment, if you're weak on the phone, peace out. If the first question the borrower asks is the rate and you give it to them right away, what have **you** gained? If you have a shopper, expect a *"thanks for the information,"* and chances are you'll never hear from that prospect again.

You are doing yourself and the potential borrower a disservice by not finding out specifically what the borrower is looking for. Instead, focus on building the relationship, go beyond just being an order taker and take the time to ask the right open-ended questions.

For example:

"What kind of debt are you looking to pay off? How long have you been paying the minimums?"

"What are the rates on those credit cards?"

"Home improvement? Great. What are you looking to add on, and how long have you been thinking about doing it? Sounds like that patio you're going to build will make the summer much more tolerable in that heat."

"Looking to buy a home? Awesome! How long have you been looking to buy, and what's your timeframe on the purchase? What type of property are you looking to get? Anything specific you're looking for with the new house?"

If you throw out a rate without pulling credit, the borrower gets what they want, and you waste your time. If a borrower refuses to talk with you about their goals, won't let you pull credit, and won't give you their financial information, then telling them a rate is just like throwing stank at a wall and hoping it sticks.

If you're giving the borrower something (your time and expertise), then the borrower should be giving you something, which is permission to access their credit. Thus, by not taking the easy way out, you start to build a relationship. Borrowers are more likely to remember you after you pull their credit than the last roll-over loan officer who just shot off a rate. If you've done your best to gain access to the borrower's credit and they still won't budge, then give them your number and tell them you wouldn't be doing your job (or fiduciary duty, if you want to get fancy-pants) to just pull their credit to find out what kind of loan they would qualify for and check in from time to time with them. Chances are you never would have gotten that loan in the first place. If you follow up with them in a week, usually they still haven't decided. Time to lock them down.

URGENCY

Maybe you have a borrower who has an 8% rate. Another may have tons of debt and have been looking into refinancing for a year but never pulled the trigger on saving a grip of cheddar. How is it possible they are still in this money-sapping situation?

The answer could be for one of several reasons. However, it's probably because the last loan officers they spoke with did not convey any urgency, so they procrastinated and then forgot about it.

Borrowers need to act now—not a week from now, not tomorrow—*now*. Getting a loan wrapped up the same day can't happen every time, especially with purchases, but a 24-hour window should be your goal. This is true even in emails. Twenty-two percent more emails are opened if the header seems urgent. Seventeen percent fewer are opened if the word in the header is "quick". Don't ask me to figure it out. I still have a hard time checking the tire pressure on my car; just a random tip.

Remember *Rocky III*? In the film, Rocky is down on himself, and Apollo Creed isn't having it. Rocky is half-assing it, and he tells Apollo that he will get it together tomorrow. You have to fight Clubber Lang, bro; get moving! Frustrated with the Italian Stallion, Apollo yells, *"There is no tomorrow! THERE IS NO TOMORROW!"* Adopt this approach with your borrowers—minus the heavy drama. Haven't seen *Rocky III*? What are you, a communist? I recently had a loan officer ask me who the Fonz was; damn, I'm getting old.

I play this clip for my loan officers for comedic value but also to prove a point. This is how you need to look at loans. If the loan makes sense, then what is your borrower waiting for? They can call back tomorrow, but the rate may be blown to the point it no longer makes sense. All sorts of outside forces can make a loan go south quickly; you can control some of them. Get the loan locked in now, and get it completed. I always let my more trepidatious borrowers know that the worst thing that can happen is that they cancel—nothing lost, nothing gained. However, the chance of them cancelling is slim once they jump on board and feel good about you.

Pressure is an art form. Master it and understand that it's necessary for borrowers that have become accustomed to not making a decision. In the end, when the loan is funded, if the loan was written correctly with the borrower's interests being met, all parties will benefit.

BENEFIT SELLING

If you don't know what benefit selling is, it's time to go back to sales school, pal. If you've been a loan officer before, then everything I'm reviewing is material you should know. However, possibly due to a complacent stretch, which happens to the best of us, you may have had a brain flush on some of these concepts.

Why would anyone want to refinance their mortgage loan? Bennies, my people! Say 'em once, say 'em twice, say 'em till you can't say 'em anymore. When the borrower leaves a conversation with you, they need to know why this loan makes sense to them. Write down five benefits before every pitch. For example:

- By including your credit card debt in your mortgage loan, you will be able to write it off in your taxes.

- You are going to save _____ a month overall and _____ over a period of five years.

- By locking this rate in now, we know that you will qualify for this purchase today.

Let's make this dream home happen without any surprises down the road.

- If we consolidate the second home equity loan, your rate will be locked. You won't have to worry about the rate going up on the equity loan despite all signs pointing to a rate increase.

- Your six credit card bills will now be consolidated into one. The hassle of having to worry about paying all six and possibly being late will no longer be an issue.

- You can take the $300 a month you are saving and put it back into the principal. By doing this, you would knock six years off your mortgage and save an estimated $73,000.

The last three minutes of your initial pitch should ALWAYS include the benefits—even if you mentioned them before. A typical loan application takes 30 to 45 minutes, and in some cases, up to three hours; much can be forgotten in that time frame.

The mortgage rate is higher than what they currently have. So what?

When giving a borrower details on a cash-out loan, I cannot stress this fact enough: If the borrower is saving money, then the rate should be almost irrelevant.

Some loan officers get stuck on the mortgage rate if it's higher than the rate the borrowers currently have. The bottom line is this: If the borrower is saving money by paying off debt, that savings will lead to a better quality of life for the borrower.

I can hear it in my sweaty nightmares: *"Well, sir, we can save you $600 a month by taking care of your credit card debt, **BUT** your rate will be going up from 3% to 5%, so not sure if that would make sense for you."*

No BUTS, and you do not decide what is right for the borrower! If the borrower can save money over all, then why does the rate matter? Replace **but** with **and your new rate will be _____**. Don't shy away from or feel guilty about the higher rate.

Some borrowers hold onto their low interest rate because they like to brag to the neighbors about it. It's an interest rate, not a Nobel Prize! What good is a low rate if it's costing the borrower money by leaving the other debt hanging out there that they could be paying off? (Rarely is there one debt.) Also, home improvement rates are typically higher, and HELOCs are adjustable and much harder to get than a refinance.

One of the best loan officers I've worked with would never back down from a rate if the loan made sense. One of his questions when facing rate blowback would be, *"Do you want your current rate? Or do you want the money and savings?"* That question presents the bottom line and a simple way to approach it. Also, if the cash-out loan is from the Federal Housing Administration (FHA) or VA, chances are that in seven months, borrowers will just flip into a streamline loan at a lower rate anyway.

A SORRY ISN'T ALWAYS NECESSARY

If processing screwed up the loan, you sent out documents that were incorrect, or you misquoted a rate, then apologize. On the flip side, if rates went up, the fees are high, or the appraisal comes in low, and you were honest about the value up front, why are you saying that you are sorry?

In these instances, it's not your fault. As a matter of fact, in some cases, it is the borrower's fault, so don't feel bad letting them know. Now, rubbing it in their face is not what I am talking about, but in the case of a higher rate, a proper response would be, *"It looks like you have been shopping around for a couple weeks. Let's make sure this we lock this rate in and get moving forward today so it doesn't happen again."*

You may be trying to avoid embarrassment by apologizing, but research shows that those who refuse to apologize for things that are not their fault maintain a greater sense of control and feel better about themselves. No one likes to leave work with nothing to show for it and feeling like a beaten mule.

When you apologize to a borrower, you give that person a sense of power, and as we have learned by now, controlling the borrower and the conversation is a major aspect of completing the loan and allowing the borrower a better quality of life.

If it is your mistake, apologize and restore the relationship. This is actually a time to show your own vulnerability. However, some things related to your company are just not in your control. If it's not your fault, you can sympathize with the borrower, but do not necessarily apologize. Work with the borrower to find a solution, and they will respect you more for it—people respect strength, not tepidness. Always try to maintain a good sense of humor throughout the conversation. Also, I beg of you on my hands and knees, never say, *"To be honest with you."* Kinda gives the impression you weren't being forthright up until that point, which, as Charles Barkley would say, is *"turrible."*

BE A VERBAL MONET

Think about what you're doing when pitching a client. If you're doing it well, you should be painting a picture that will stick in their brain. This picture can be painted using any benefits, some of which we went over earlier.

Have borrowers visualize what it will be like to rip up those high-interest credit card debts and to have less stress. Maybe they're building a pool. The kids are really going to dig that. A pool should make for some good parties with all their friends, especially during those steamy summers.

Don't stop when you find out what they need the money for; have them form a mental image of the result by helping them anticipate what will happen once the loan is completed. *"The sooner we get started, the sooner you'll be drinking a cold one in the shade on your new patio."*

TAKEAWAYS

1. Knowing your product will sell more loans, so continue to learn.

2. The loan makes sense, so assume they want it until they tell you they don't, then ask open-ended questions to find out why.

3. Hold a borrower's hand and lead the way; people steer toward leaders, not followers.

Chapter 3

ATTITUDE

Toward what kind of people do you navigate?

My guess is that if you have a friend who is always negative and bitching, then you probably skip out on them sometimes, because what fun is it hanging around a whiny pain in the keister? Why would it be any different when you're on the phone with a borrower?

BE POSITIVE

You are the biggest part of your reality. Whether that reality is happy, sad, mad, or glad, it lies in your hands. It's impossible to be positive 100% of the time, but be cognizant of the conversations you are having as well. When it may be taking a turn to the dark side, flip it.

Weather sucks over there? Well, it should clear up in a few days, and your borrower may be able to get out for a hike. The loan processing is terrible? Nice thing is that when the loan is wrapped up, the struggles will be worth it and then some.

Positivity is the same in phone sales as it is in life. People navigate toward positivity and veer away from negativity. Being positive can disarm even the crankiest borrower. You don't know their back-story, and this can be particularly true with a veteran who may be rough up front. When that information is conveyed through trust and open-ended questions, typically it's a *"Now I get it"* moment when you understand why the borrower may have been fussy.

We've all had that initial call with a client where the borrower was slightly disrespectful. However, those of us who persevered with those clients sometimes discovered that inside that hard candy shell was a gooey niceness, and they turned out to be a client for life. Always try to keep a cool demeanor regardless of the circumstances. However, when slight disrespect turns to straight-up abuse, give them one more chance, and then it's time to move on.

Recently, I witnessed a top loan officer who'd had a bad month. He blamed it on everyone but himself. That being said, processing did turn some of his deals into fish chum. The problem was that he couldn't get past it. For the next four months, he constantly fought with processing, earning a reputation for being a pain, and his production continued to go downhill. He ended up on the chopping block because his negative blame-game was affecting not only his production but his life in general. Every day is a new day; don't drag yesterday's nonsense into today's production. Life is too short. If you are in the office and frustrated, take a quick walk around the block and shake it off.

Word of advice: NEVER get into a pissing match with anyone in your company. You may win the battle, but you will lose the war. If you start calling out processors or underwriters, they'll remember who you are, and you may find that, shocker, your files for some wacky reason are moving slower than Congress. They're human, too. If you got verbally shredded by someone, would you expedite their files? I recommend the honey/vinegar theory in this situation. The best response is to bite your tongue and find a solution. I do simple tokens of my appreciation such as buying them a pizza. It works, no doubt.

Listen, I'm no positive Pistol Pete 24/7. When I realize that I'm going down that dark road, I try to practice what I preach and get it together. No one benefits from being negative—not you, not your borrower, and not the poor schmuck sitting in the cube farm next to you who has to listen to your pessimism all day. The least valuable person in a company finds problems and complains about them; the most valuable finds solutions to those problems. Same thing with life. Look for the people at work who will motivate you and make you better.

Keeping with the positive theme, here are some fun-time sales facts that may surprise you:

- A little over 12% of all jobs in the USA are in sales.

- Top sales producers outperform average producers by 2:1 and low producers by 10:1.

- If you follow up with web leads within five minutes, you're nine times more likely to convert them.

- Eighty-five percent of customers report being dissatisfied with their phone experiences.

We've all spoken on the phone with salespeople who are way too perky. We just want to tell them to zipit.com. The exchange comes off as a fake mess, and we can't wait to get off the phone with that type of salesperson or customer service rep.

On the opposite side are the negative people who make you want to walk to the filled tub with a plugged-in toaster. As a loan officer, your job is to know when to tone it down and when to turn it on.

Asking borrowers regulatory questions like *"Are you Hispanic or non-Hispanic?"* is not exciting. Asking them if they have a second mortgage isn't going to get anyone to leap out their chair with reckless abandon. Asking them if they are male, female, or both almost always provides some comic relief but doesn't affect the borrower. What **is** exciting is benefits and urgency. Benefits, urgency, and faith in you working hard for them is what you want to leave with your borrower.

Sound and be passionate about the savings or other positives that await borrowers. If you aren't excited about what you're looking to achieve for the borrower, then how is the borrower going to be excited?

I've listened to thousands of sales calls. I've heard loan officers almost sound depressed when a borrower is saving a grand a month. *"It's a damned grand a month, man, and this guy is on a fixed income.*

Get pumped!" If it's a purchase, *"Call me back when you find a place,"* is unacceptable. Set timelines and let them know through actions that they are lucky you are their loan officer. On the other end of the spectrum, I get a kick out of the deals where the borrower is saving thirty bucks and the loan officer makes it seem like a thousand. Excitement is contagious; project excitement, and most likely, the borrower will feed off of it.

Regarding attitude, try to do something productive BEFORE you get to work. For instance, on weekdays, I wake up around 5 a.m. I go to the gym, then head to work and am usually the first one in the building. I've accomplished a lot before most people's peepers have opened, and my early productivity generates a generally positive attitude throughout the day. Generally ;-).

If you're thinking you could never be productive before the time you normally start work, change your mindset. I didn't think early morning activity was something I would be doing either. Recently, a pal said I was nuts and that she could never roll out of bed that early. We now meet at the gym almost every day around 5:30 a.m. Typically, she beats me there and can't imagine not doing it now. Try and get out of your comfort zone.

If the early workout is too much, do something simple like cooking a good breakfast or making your bed. The key is discipline, the feeling that you have completed a task early. That feeling gets the blood flowing so that when you walk into work, you'll be ready to kick some butt. Daily patterns are good for the mind: They suppress chaos, and we all know trying to fund loans provides enough chaos to go around.

EMBRACE THE AWKWARDNESS

I was reminded of embracing the awkwardness when about a year ago I had to sleep on an inflatable bed and had none of my clothes for 12 days. I had started a new opportunity in a new state, and I felt like I was headed to Mars. Going from San Diego to El Paso can do that to a fella. Movers said it would be three days—not a chance. That inflatable bed was no treat for 11 days; however, the move turned out to be such a comedy of errors, it was laughable. I was whining about it but then decided, what good is this? Might as well roll with the punches and embrace the nonsense.

In this move, I was involved in possibly growing a new call center for 300 to 400 loan officers, all of whom had no experience in mortgages. To get to be rock stars, they had to do uncomfortable work like mock loans on a whiteboard in front of 15 sets of eyes. Most were not fans and did not like to be called on. Who would?

However, in just two weeks, I saw major and continuous improvement. The experience helped them get to the point where they quickly gained tons of confidence and surpassed some of the successful seasoned loan officers. To look in the crowd while scenarios went up on the board and to see the confusion in their eyes turn to understanding before they attacked them was awesome. Tip o' the hat to my El Paso peeps, "The Real OG's."

Once you have a working knowledge of the mortgage process, performing the same routine day after day without learning much is easy. The true pros will always strive to gain knowledge, to learn new technology and sales skills, and to try to grow every day. Whether you have been in the industry for 15 days or 40 years, ALWAYS come in with a thirst for knowledge, recognize any gap in your game, and go get you some!

TAKEAWAYS

1. Always keeping it positive at work isn't easy, but optimism will lead to a happier environment, and your borrowers will pick up on it.

2. Always treat your coworkers with respect, even if you know they're wrong. Sending a snarky e-mail might make you feel good for about one minute, but the price you pay may be long-term.

3. Don't lose sight of what you're doing for borrowers: You're saving them money and possibly changing their lives dramatically.

4. If you are learning new concepts and it is uncomfortable, you aren't doing something wrong but quite the opposite. Continue to learn and grow.

QUOTES

"It is not your customer's job to remember you. It is your obligation and responsibility to make sure they don't have the chance to forget you." – Patricia Fripp

"Lack of direction, not lack of time, is the problem. We all have 24-hour days." – Zig Ziglar

"Always do your best. What you plant now, you will harvest later." – O. G. Mandino

"Motivation will almost always beat mere talent." – Norman Ralph Augustine

Chapter 4

DON'T PHONE IT IN

You can only succeed if you show up—both physically and mentally. Everyone is going to have good and bad days; however, if you consistently try to work hard and cultivate drive, the rest should fall into place. Rise and grind!

Have you even been totally engaged with your feet kicked up on the desk? Focus on the call. Seriously.

I want to rip out what's left of my hair out when I see someone looking on their computer to see what's on Netflix tonight while they are pitching a borrower. Hundreds if not thousands of dollars are on the line for both parties, and they are checking to see if a new episode of *Ozark* is on tonight? Listen to your borrowers and focus on the task at hand for lordy's sakes, which includes not being an order taker and making sure to ask open-ended questions. When they ask you questions, keep your answers brief—the more you talk, the more they will get confused and forget what you are trying to tell them. Protect your time—you only have so many hours in the day.

You have your script or pitch; you know what you want to say. How about what **they** want to say? With just a little feedback, you can figure out what the borrower wants. The call isn't about you getting through your presentation. The conversation should be fluent and open.

One loan officer I was rooting for followed directions to a T. She would read the script, was conscientious, had a great attitude, and was a great learner. Nevertheless, she was constantly at the bottom of the pile. Why? Because she was so focused on telling the borrower what we were offering that she didn't listen to what the borrower was looking to do. **What is the borrower trying to tell you, and what are they not telling you?** Many times, a borrower does not want you to know the trouble they are in or challenges they may be facing. It's your job to find the issues. Sell with questions, not answers.

Phone sales, in some ways, are more difficult than face-to-face sales. All you have is the borrower's voice to go on and vice versa. However, ways exist to bring phone sales closer to face-to-face meetings. Listen to what's stressing borrowers, what's relaxing them, etc.

If borrowers start talking about a busted ex who disappeared and was nice enough to leave them with a stack of bills, ask how much the bills were, how long they've been paying them, and what the interest rates are. Let them know, *"Together, we will work to find a resolution."* Reassure and empathize with them.

"Sounds like a bad situation, and I know it's been rough. However, I'm glad we're talking because we're going to take care of those bills with a cash-out refinance, and you can put these issues in the past very soon."

Seventy percent of people make purchasing decisions to solve problems. Thirty percent make purchasing decisions to gain something. What does this mean to you? Understanding the borrower's issues in some cases is more important than talking about the benefits.

Peel that onion. Shuck that corn. (OK, I am out of lame metaphors.) Find out what's behind those borrowers' words. They'd like to get $20k back? Or maybe they want to pay off debt. For some loan officers, that's where it ends. Keep it going. *"How long have you had that debt? Are you paying just the minimums? Wow. Okay, by my calculations it looks like it's going to take you six years to get these credit cards paid off, and you can't write the interest off, either, like you would be able to in a debt-consolidation refinance. What are the interest rates on these credit cards? 15%? Typically, the rates only go up. I'm glad we're talking so we can resolve this."*

When a borrower knows you're listening to what they are saying and you're not just an order-taking robot, they will open up and be more willing to give you the information you need. (Speaking of AI, Space X CEO Elon Musk said he is almost positive that we will be slaves to the androids in the future, so enjoy yourself while you still can.) As a loan officer, I would pull up a credit card calculator and show them the pain of the situation. Some borrowers have no idea how long it takes to pay off credit card debt, and that realization of finding out how long it takes can be a serious wake-up call.

One way to let borrowers know that you're listening is to repeat some of the more important points they've mentioned and inject your own confident opinion on them. *"This debt occurred when your mom got sick, and you did the right thing in taking care of her. Now, it's time to get you moving forward again by handling this debt and removing the burden."*

Repeating their issues is important because you are clarifying their needs, and they know you are listening and care. If they agree with what they need to do, then they should move forward with the loan.

SET A SPECIFIC TIME TO CALL BACK

"I'll give you a call this afternoon" won't cut it. You think afternoon is one o'clock, and they think it's four. Set a specific time. Even if it's only an hour

away, don't tell them you will call in an hour: People remember specifics, not generalities. By setting a specific time, you accomplish several things. First, you get a small commitment from the potential borrower. (In fact, closing a loan is the result of a set of small commitments.) Second, setting a specific time shows that you're a busy professional who can't call any time during the day. Third, you leave the reason for the next call. Simply saying *"I'll follow up with you tomorrow"* doesn't mean squat. Why are you following up with them tomorrow? You're following up with them tomorrow to instruct them on the next move; let them know your expectations.

You may also want to send them an e-mail a few hours in advance to remind them. Remember, you're running the show. If borrowers don't want to set aside a specific time, that's most likely a sign that they're not truly interested. Find out why; keep digging in.

Setting a specific callback time also ties into urgency. If, according to you, any time during the day is fine for a callback, then any time during the month to move forward must be fine, which it's not. If a borrower knows you're a busy professional, they should be there to take the call. If it's missed, and your initial conversation was solid, typically they will feel a bit guilty about missing the call, which can work in your favor. Always thank people for their time and show respect for it. Never go into a call not knowing what your goal is; always be prepared. Finally, if you are leaving a message, never say you are "checking in"—that reeks of desperation. Instead, leave a message with a game plan such as, *"Rates are going up; you will have to close the file, and they will be losing money if you do,"* etc. Again, pressure is not necessarily negative.

WRITE DOWN THE SMALL STUFF

Does your borrower have to get off the phone to take his daughter to a soccer game? Write down the anecdotes. The next time you talk with him, ask how the game went. The boss is up in their grill? In the follow-up call, you'll want to ask if the boss has chilled out yet. Build a relationship.

Getting personal with borrowers lets them know that you're a human being. Being perceived as flesh and blood is especially important with rate shoppers. If they're talking with five salespeople all offering similar programs but just tossing out numbers, they're going to remember you.

One study says that 63% of all borrowers remember the stories that were told, and 5% remember statistics. Now, this in no way is to say just yap for an hour about the great time you had at Lake Titicaca and not tell them the benefits of the loan, but you get the idea.

With that being said, know when to say when. Some borrowers can just drone on about anything and everything. Be courteous at all times, but when the conversation gets to a point where you need to move forward, don't feel bad about diverting back to the loan.

We all at some point have gone with the salesperson who seemed to be involved in the conversation and seemed to care about our end-result, even if the terms may have been slightly more monetarily than the competition's—reason being they seemed to understand us more than the person who was just throwing out stats.

TELL THEM TO GRAB A PEN AND PAPER

There are many reasons for this, so let's go over a few. First of all, when it comes to a significant other being involved, much gets lost in translation when they are trying to explain the conversation you had with them. If you cannot get the other borrower on the phone, which should be your first goal, they need to write down what you went over. I'm not talking about your name and number after a pitch,

I am talking about having them write specific details about the loan.

It is especially powerful when you go over their current debt situation. Let's say they have six credit cards that are being paid off. Have your borrower draw a line down the middle of the paper and write down each individual card with the interest rate and the minimum payment. Add them up and give them the estimated timeframe it will take to pay off that debt. Then on the other side of the line, give them the savings, both short- and long-term, as well as the other benefits this loan provides. Take that extra few minutes. Borrowers forget like we do; for those that have been in the business, we have all had borrowers that seem to be ecstatic with the benefits of a loan who we never hear from again. Chances are they forgot about the benefits and were talked out of the loan by a spouse or friend. When they write the benefits down, much less can get lost in translation, and they can reference their notes if any questions arise when you are not available to answer them.

Also, as I went over earlier with regard to guidelines and memory, these benefits will leave more of an imprint on their cabeza.

TIMELINES

Borrowers procrastinate, and they lose money in doing so. A guy sitting on the fence can lose hundreds if not thousands of dollars in a few months because of rising rates or other yet-to-arise issues. Let them know that. Have them set a timeline, and if they don't want to decide today, have them decide within twenty-four hours. If they are not willing to do that, then they may not be serious about getting this done. Again, find out why.

Back in my loan officer days, a borrower called me back a week after our conversation and went ballistic because the rates had gone up and we hadn't locked in the earlier rate. If I hadn't advised her to lock in the rate during our conversation the week earlier, she would have had every right to be upset. I had told her, but of course, she was still unhappy. Unless you want to be unhappy again next week, let's lock it in now. Be firm yet empathetic.

MONETIZE IT

I always scratch my head when the same borrowers who think that $100 on a no-cost mortgage loan isn't worth it will spend an hour on the phone haggling with AT&T to save $10 on their cell phone bill. Find out when they started considering a loan. Then let them know how much they would have saved if they had moved forward from that point. If they wait, tell them how much money they'll be losing for each day that they wait. For instance, "Mr. Borrower, we are saving you $440 a month on this loan. Every week we hold off on moving forward is going to cost you $102, so let's get this done today so we can start the savings ASAP."

DON'T OFFER TOO MANY OPTIONS

Try to keep options for the borrower to two. Any more can lead to confusion and procrastination. Break it down. Let's say they want to look at a 30- and a 15-year term. Show them what that is with costs. Now, they like the 15-year but don't want to pay costs, so show them the 15-year cost vs. no cost. Furthermore, if a borrower hesitates about what they want to do, assure them that they can change the terms of the loan during the process. Just ask what seems to make the most sense of the options given. *"Okay, let's move forward with this 30-year loan. Remember, we can change the terms during the process, and it's no hassle at all."*

TAKEAWAYS

1. Dig into the borrower's needs, get engaged, and make sure the borrower is engaged. Pay attention to what is going on in the borrower's life other than just the loan. The more you know, the more you can assist the borrower.

2. Respect the borrower's time, and make them aware that you respect their time.

3. Set specific follow-up times. Following a script is always recommended, but you need to forge your own path during the conversation so you don't sound like C-3PO.

4. Break down the daily or weekly savings or benefits if they want to hold off on moving forward and try not to confuse them with too many loan options.

Chapter 5

IT IS WHAT YOU MAKE IT

F act: The most successful salespeople in the world don't sit by and wait for the phone to ring. They hunt. Staring down the barrel of a phone receiver can be daunting, but what's the worst that can happen? A potential or past borrower tells you to stick it? That makes for good office conversation, so who cares?

To quote from one of my favorite films, *Glengarry Glen Ross*, *"You know what it takes to sell real estate? It takes brass balls."* Let's be real—you need alligator-thick skin in this industry to succeed.

What do you have to lose? If you don't pick up that phone, you're doing nothing but losing money. If you're in an outbound campaign, dial often and dial hard. Don't dial to meet dial quotas; dial to be successful. It's a simple numbers game: more dials, more contacts, more money in your bank account. Sales are incremental. A small extra effort daily will lead to huge gains at the end of the month or year.

Pay attention to the wins and losses. How did you get that outbound application, and how did you lose it? Over time, you should be able to figure out what works and what doesn't. Just hanging up and moving to the next call without reflection results in no improvement.

GET IT DONE

Learn from those who are more successful than you. A line from political commentator Ben Shapiro, "Facts don't care about your feelings," rings true here. If someone is out-producing you, don't snowflake out and make excuses; do something about it. Don't let your ego prevent you from asking those successful people questions on how to get where you want to be.

So far, what I have gone over contains nothing mind-blowing. In a modern environment, this information presents sales skills that in some cases have been tried and proven true for not hundreds but thousands of years before a mortgage ever existed. One of the best things about mortgage sales is that you can come from any walk of life and be a pro if you just follow some relatively simple guides and work hard. Think about it—in no other profession can you walk through the door and make six figures almost immediately. For instance,

I graduated with a degree in industrial sociology—basically useless, but I did learn that life is a stage! Shout out to the theory of dramaturgy. I had a hell of a good time in college, though.

Mortgage sales takes a bit of understanding about how the human mind works and then using that knowledge to your advantage but in the end benefitting the borrower. It's not manipulation—you're getting people what they want, though they may not know it at the time. Look at it this way: If you were paying 20% on a credit card for years and then someone told you that a 4% rate was available, *plus* you could write off the interest, wouldn't that sound pretty kick-ass? Well, this is what we do. Delivered properly with all the pieces of the puzzle in place, everyone wins.

YOU DON'T WORK AT FACEBOOK

If you're at work, then work. The games on your

phone or social networks aren't going anywhere; besides, they are mining all your data and using it for nefarious purposes. To think you're being sneaky by not working hard helps no one, least of all you.

Call centers can be a grind, but you need to embrace the process. One specific follow-up time can lead to one more credit pull that can lead to one more application. Doing all the small stuff over and over makes the big stuff happen.

Think of what wasting just two hours a day does over time. That's one full workday per week and around one week per month. We all need time to slow down and take a breath; however, if you think you have nothing to do, then *find* something to do. E-mail old clients. Look through appraisals. Find out something new about the industry you call a career. (At the end of this book, you'll find several links that can keep you up to date on the mortgage industry.)

Studies show that 33% of an average salesperson's time is spent selling. Imagine if you were able to add just 5% a day to that, and then shoot for 10%. The difference in production at year's end would be astronomical.

If your boss walks by and the computer screen goes from Instagram to a 1003, you aren't fooling anyone. If you find yourself repeating this scene throughout the day, then something is wrong on your end.

Stay productive whenever possible. If you truly have nothing to do, then ask your boss what you can do to improve. If they are worth their salt, they will have some ideas for you that will only make you better and more satisfied. You can check up on Kate's best-ever wine tasting trip on Lamebook later. (She was probably BSing about how awesome it was anyway; the whole trip was a train wreck because Sheila got drunk again and was talking smack about Debra's philandering husband.)

Don't be a drone and sit down, do your work, and leave. You don't work for the DMV and don't get paid like you do. Learn one thing a day—imagine the knowledge reimbursement that will pay weekly, monthly, and yearly. One guideline, one sales tip, one anything that will make you better doesn't take long. Seriously, five minutes. Set up a reminder in Outlook and do it daily.

Listen and learn from the best. Frustration will occur when success is fleeting (if you truly want to be successful.) Excuses are easy: The leads blow, management doesn't know what they're doing, the processing team in Bangladesh doesn't speak English, etc. If someone else in the office is successful, then you can be, too. If someone else who has that success is cool, hip, rad, dope, sweet, or tight (trying to cover all demographics) enough to let you know what their keys to success are, emulate them until you find your own path.

Self-evaluation is only easy when you're patting yourself on the back for a job well done. No one likes to face their weaknesses, but unless you want to never improve, self-evaluation is an absolute must. Listening to your calls can be painful. That said, I have never reviewed a call with someone who didn't learn from it. NEVER. Now, whether you use that information or forget about it when you walk out the door is up to you.

Think of every legendary sports star you know in recent history. (I say *recent* because Babe Ruth was just a big boozing womanizer who somehow managed to continually crush a baseball.) Back to more somewhat more recent stars like LeBron, Gretzky, Jordan, and Brady. Even if they're the best at what they do, constant improvement is necessary. They were and are never happy being number one because they want to stay on top of the pile. On the flip side, think of the athletes who had everything going for them and got complacent. The only time you ever hear from them is on some tragic ESPN 30 for 30 series. I'm looking at you, Jamarcus Russell. However, being a **FORMER** Chargers fan, I would like to thank him for replacing Ryan Leaf as the worst bust of all time. When they left for LA, no mas Los Chargers para mi, but I digress.

I've often looked over the sea of faces during a training and seen glossed-over eyes with a *"just get this over with"* look. It's a bad look, especially because my meetings are always action-packed, (cough, ahem). When I hear the exact opposite of something I just went over on the very next call from a loan officer, it indicates to me that they think they have nothing more to learn or they don't agree, at which point we should discuss. Take notes. Stick Post-its on your computer to remind you about key areas.

Remember, management or trainers can give you advice until their faces turn blue, but it's up to you to follow their instructions. Your trainers/ managers want you to succeed. If you can't take one thing away from the training that will improve your current production, then that is on management.

Don't feel bad if you are struggling or don't understand something. Let your manager know, because that is one of many reasons they are there. If they are worth their salt, they will be happy to help.

TAKEAWAYS

1. The script is important, but don't be a drone. Go outside the script and ask relevant questions to find more benefits.

2. When you're at work, work! Adding just a bit of that time spent on non–work-related

items to your work will make a huge difference when you see your year-end W-2.

3. If others in the office are successful, then you can be, too. Find out what they're doing that you aren't. Put your ego in check.

Chapter 6

COMMON REBUTTALS

Although you'll face many, the following rebuttals are the ones you'll hear 80% of the time.

Many variations exist, but this list is a good start. If you approach these rebuttals with confidence and if you understand that rebuttals are typically buying signals, once you answer, soon it will be time for you to get "appy."

- **I want to see if rates get better.**

  LOAN OFFICER: *"Rates are still at near-record lows. Since the election of 2016 (current example obviously; when Bieber is president in 2040, we shall see), rates have been on an upward trend, so sitting on the sidelines may cost you thousands. Let's lock in this rate now. If for some reason rates do dip, which is doubtful, we should be able to make that adjustment."*

- **I need to speak with my spouse.**

  LOAN OFFICER: *"I completely understand. I'm not looking to get anyone in the doghouse, but can you think of any reason why he/she would not want to save_____ (whatever the benefit is)?"*

  BORROWER 1: *"No."*

  LOAN OFFICER: *"Well then, let's get the rate locked in while we know it still makes sense. This way he/she can have the details of the loan to review, and I will get them over today."*

BORROWER 2: *"Yes."*

LOAN OFFICER: *"All right. Do you mind if I ask why he/she wouldn't want to save _____ every month and _____ over five years?"*

If the borrower says the spouse will have a problem, they probably still have concerns, and you can find out what they are.

- **I'm just looking for a home equity loan.**

  There are several ways to approach this, but here are two:

  LOAN OFFICER: *"If you're planning on selling the property in the next year or two, the home equity line of credit rate might make sense if it is under what a fixed refinance rate would be. However, if you plan on staying in the property for more than a couple of years, the home equity line of credit is always some form of an adjustable and/or an interest-only loan, which can cause issues if it rises. Rates are rising, and the average rate for a HELOC over the last 10 has been over 6%."*

LOAN OFFICER: *"If you're staying in the house more than a couple of years, the fixed rate, in my opinion, is where you want to be. Who knows where that HELOC will be in a year or two?"*

- **Why are the closing costs so high?**
  LOAN OFFICER: *"We give you the option of having closing costs for a lower rate or a no-cost loan with a higher rate. I recommend paying the fees if you plan on staying in the house for more than five years. If not, do the no-cost loan. Which makes more sense for you?"*

- **I need to think about it.**
  LOAN OFFICER: *"Okay, can you let me know what your concerns are?"*
  (If none) LOAN OFFICER: *"The last thing I would want to have happen is for you to call me back in a week and find that the rate has gone up. I don't expect these rates to come back to this level*

for a very long time. If it makes sense now, it will probably make sense tomorrow, so let's get this locked in now. If down the line, for whatever reason, you decide not to move forward, we can cancel, but I don't think that's going to be the case based on the amount we're saving you." (Go over savings and benefits again.)

- **I don't want you to pull my credit.**

  LOAN OFFICER: *"Do you plan on making any big purchases in the next 45 days that would require your credit score?"*

  BORROWER: *"No."*

  LOAN OFFICER: *"The reason that you have good credit is to save you money. Chances are this loan is one of the biggest opportunities you may ever have to do that. While I can't talk specifically about the effect this loan will have on your credit for regulatory purposes, I can tell you from looking at your credit profile that the effect will be temporary—about 60 to 90 days—before the small hit disappears."*

LOAN OFFICER: *"If this is something you're serious about, no lender worth his salt will try to give you an accurate payment and interest rate without taking a look at your credit, so that's something that needs to be done."*

Try to keep every rebuttal concise. Try not to sound defensive or too aggressive. A good way to approach hesitant people is to break out those loan benefits again.

CONCLUSION

B y now, you've figured out that mortgage call center sales can be difficult for a variety of reasons. Still, the pathway to success is right in front of you. Expect to work hard to get there. The truth is, I've known some great people who just aren't cut out for mortgage sales. I've also seen plenty of people who were in the production death spiral when, without warning, the light bulb went on and the crushing began. Sell yourself first, and you can sell anything. If you aren't where you need to be with production, typically it just takes simple changes in your sales game. The plan to succeed should already be laid out; it just needs to be followed.

One example was a loan officer who completely turned his game around by telling the borrower that he needed the signed documents back that day. Previously, he had said 72 hours. He told me, "I finally just did what you were telling me to do."

His docs-back percentage went up 50%—no joke. Better late than never, I guess. Simple concepts like urgency, assumption, and knowing your product make the difference. In addition, your managers are paid to make you better, and you have plenty of information available to improve your game. If your company doesn't do a good job of providing information, I just gave you a decent roadmap.

For those who are brand new, I hope that you will start off on fire and build your lucrative careers. For those who have been in the game for a while, I hope you've found a few nuggets that will add to your skill set. On one call, a borrower will scream at you because the processing is miserable. On the next call, a borrower will cry because you funded the loan, kept the electricity on, and changed their lives. Try not to get too low or too high, but take time to examine the losses and appreciate the wins. Get pumped because you're in a profession where the sky is the limit and the amount of money you can make is extraordinary. You can make a positive change in people's lives. There is a principle of unequal distribution, even in animals—someone will always come out on top, so why can't you be the leader of the pack? If you have the passion and the drive, nothing will stand in your way.

Now fire up that phone and get to selling!

REFERENCES

http://www.mortgagenewsdaily.com/

https://www.finviz.com

https://www.benefits.va.gov/homeloans/

https://www.fha.com/

https://www.zillow.com/mortgage-calculator/

https://www.nationalmortgagenews.com/

https://www.fanniemae.com/singlefamily

http://www.freddiemac.com/

Made in the USA
Las Vegas, NV
27 October 2021